How to Draw
SEA CREATURES

Learn to draw **20** ocean animals,
step by easy step, shape by simple shape!

Illustrated by Russell Farrell

Getting Started

When you look closely at the drawings in this book, you'll notice that they're made up of basic shapes, such as circles, triangles, and rectangles. To draw all these underwater creatures, just start with simple shapes as you see here. It's easy and fun!

Circles
are used to draw eyes, heads, and round bodies.

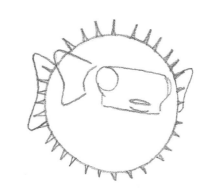

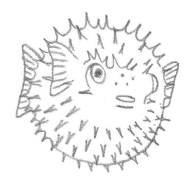

Ovals
are good for drawing sea creature profiles.

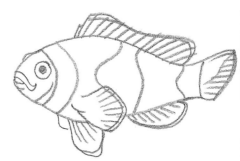

Triangles
are best for drawing the heads of some fish.

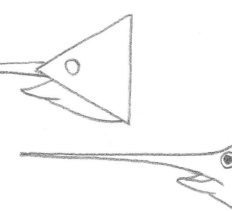

TIPS

There's more than one way to bring your ocean friends to life on paper—you can use crayons, markers, or pencils. Just be sure you have blue, green, and purple, plus yellow and orange.

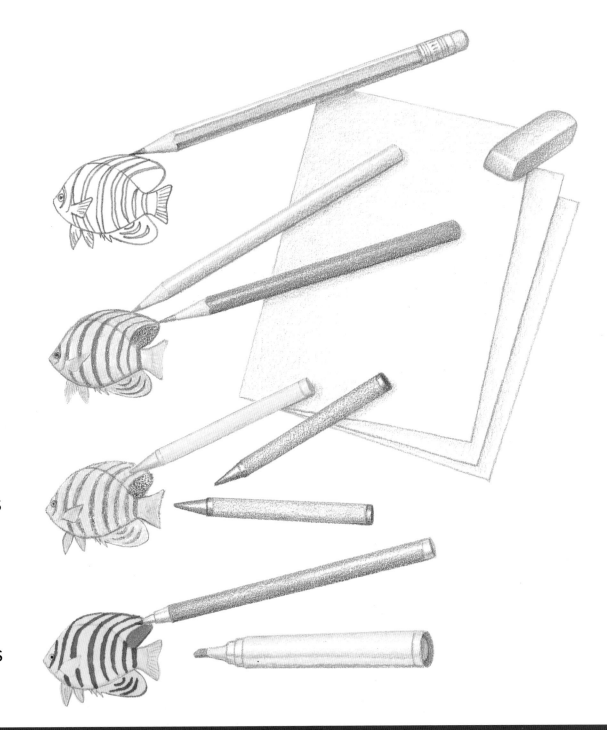

Pencils

Crayons

Markers

PUffer

The body of the puffer is one of the simplest shapes of all sea creatures—its body is nearly a perfect circle!

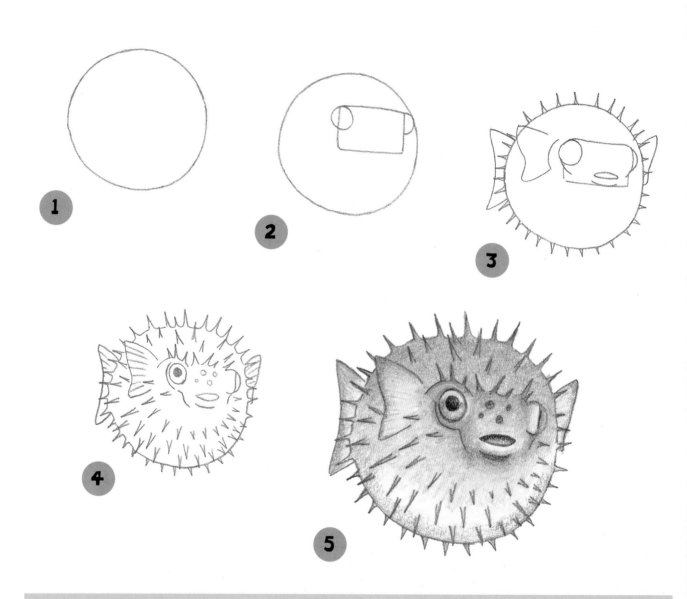

FUN FACT

With all the predators in the ocean, many fish have adapted unique ways to defend themselves. The puffer (also called the "blowfish" or "swellfish") can fill itself up with air or water to become a round, spiky ball, making it very difficult for a predator to swallow!

ANGELFISH

An elegant creature, this tropical fish
is known for its vibrant stripes.

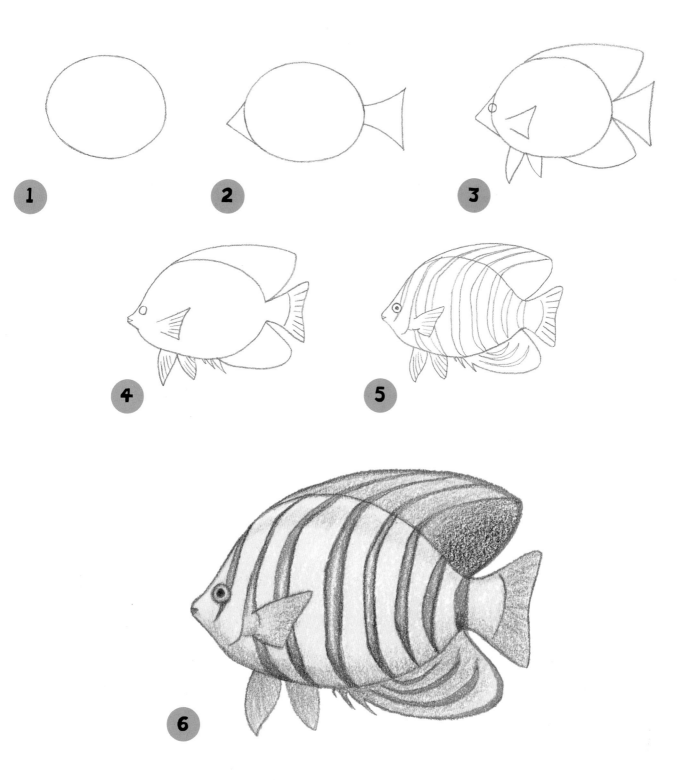

Harp Seal

Draw this sweet baby harp seal with rounded, gently curving lines and big, dark "puppy-dog" eyes.

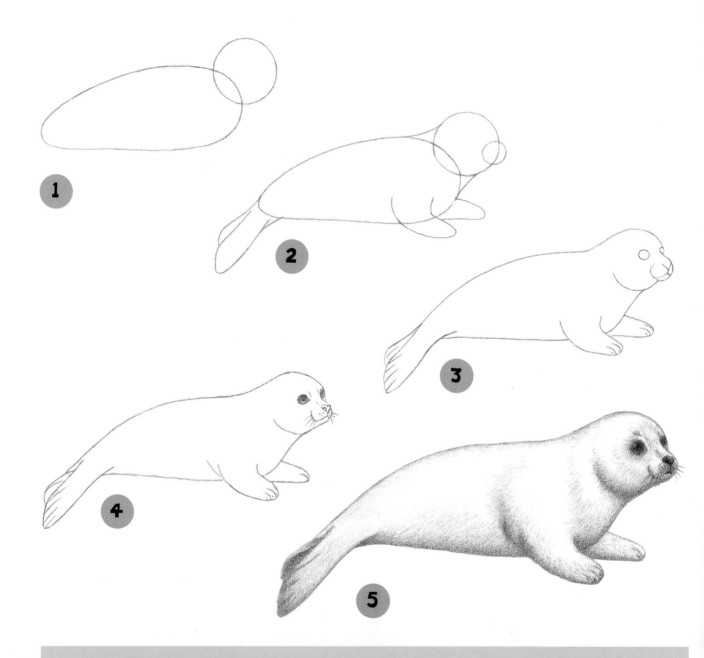

sea star

Start drawing this sea animal with simple circles! Then add five triangular arms to create the star shape.

HUMPBACK WHALE

Weighing in at **2** tons, the humpback is
a whale of a creature—its huge fins are nearly
one-third as long as its body!

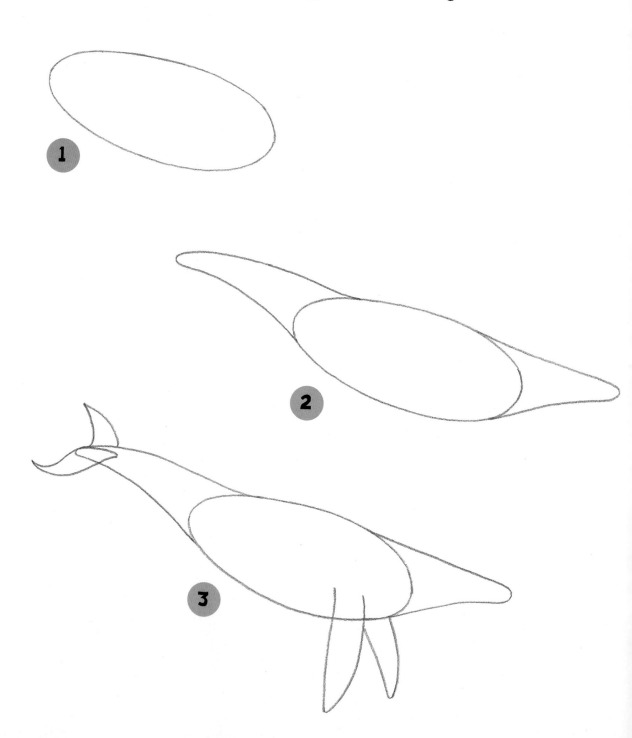

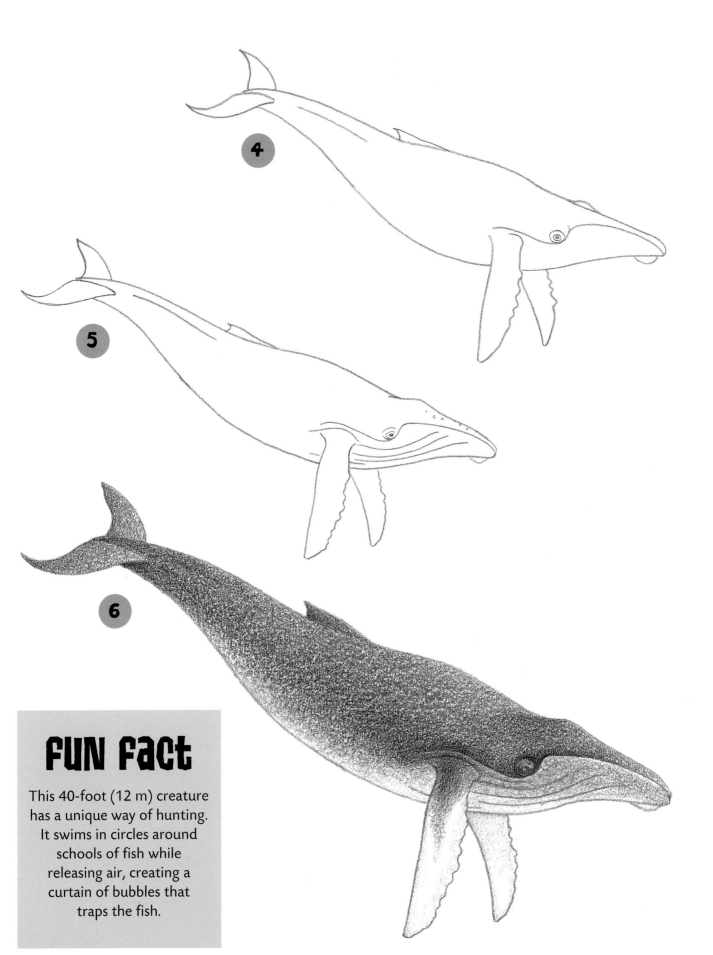

FUN FACT

This 40-foot (12 m) creature has a unique way of hunting. It swims in circles around schools of fish while releasing air, creating a curtain of bubbles that traps the fish.

sea otter

This cute critter has webbed back feet, tiny ears, a foot-long tail, and thick brown fur.

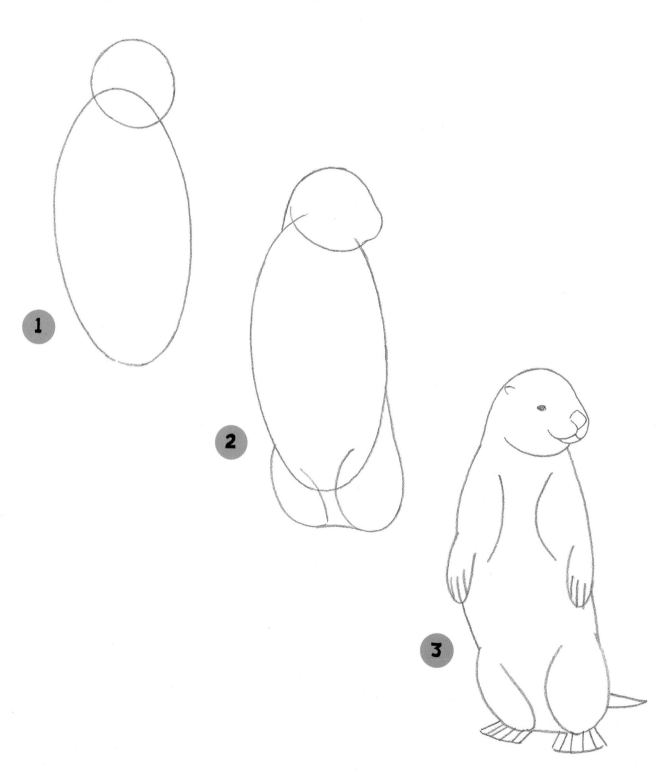

CLOWN FiSH

A popular saltwater aquarium creature, the eye-catching clown fish sports bright gold bands.

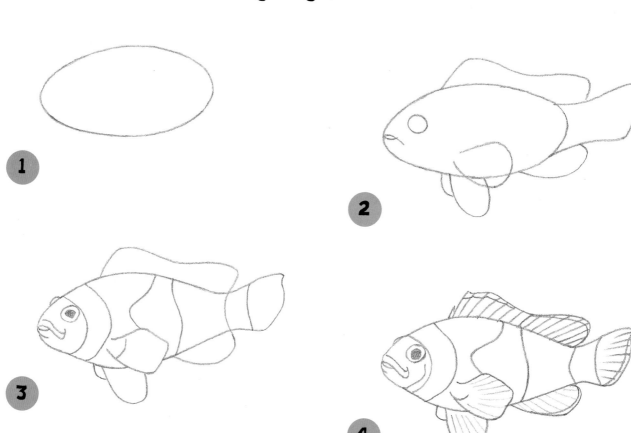

FUN Fact

The clown fish and sea anemone (an animal on the seafloor that resembles a flower) depend on one another for survival. The clown fish hides among the stinging tentacles of the anemone for protection from predators. While it's there, it eats algae and debris, cleaning the anemone.

stingray

A bottom-dweller, the stingray has a thin, flat body that allows it to both hide in the sand and glide through the water.

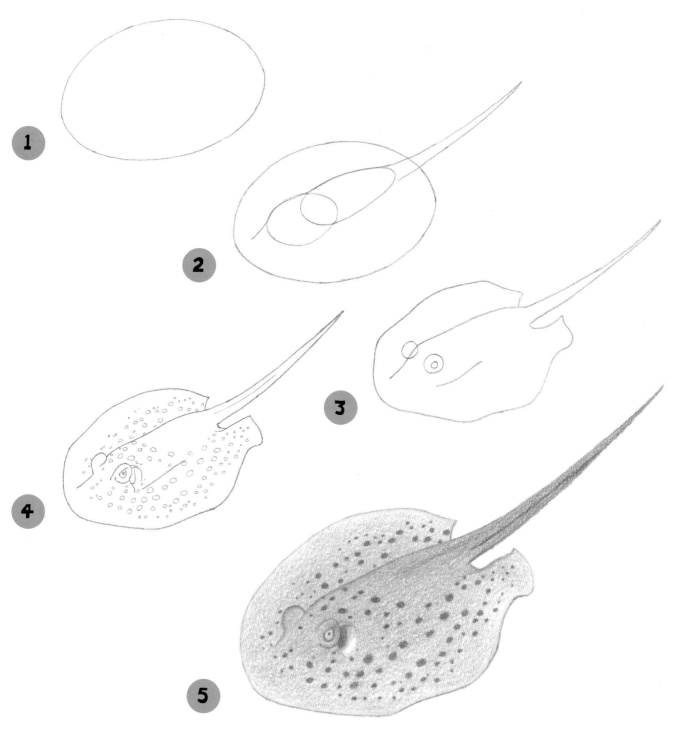

Great White Shark

The most feared of all sharks, this predator has a long, pointed snout and razor-sharp, triangular teeth.

OCEAN BASICS
There are four major oceans on Earth. From largest to smallest, they are the Pacific Ocean, the Atlantic Ocean, the Indian Ocean, and the Arctic Ocean.

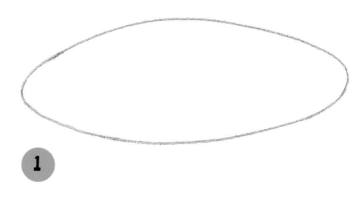

1

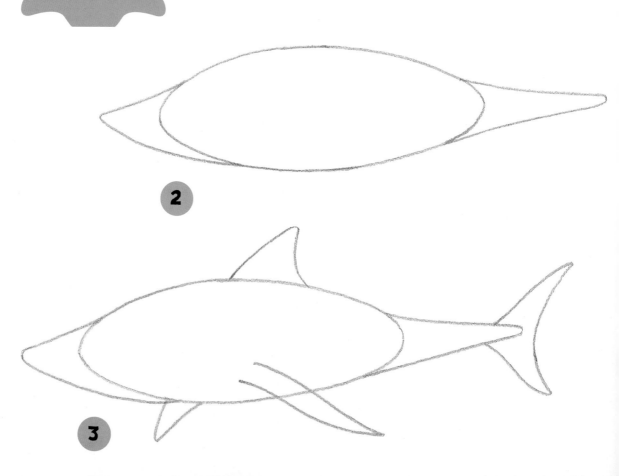

2

3

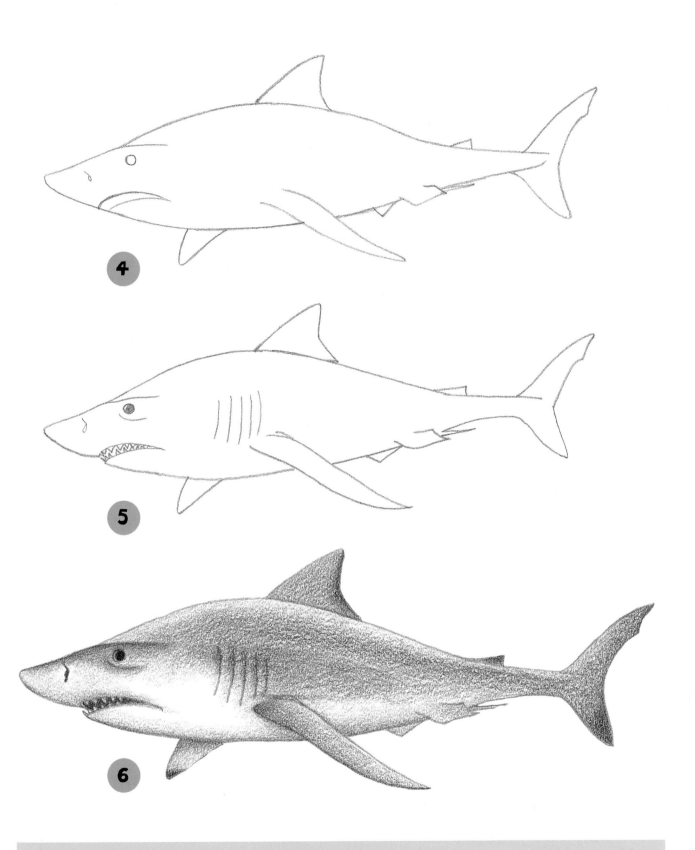

4

5

6

FUN FACT

A great white has about 3,000 jagged teeth arranged in several rows. The shark uses only the first two rows for capturing prey; the rest of the teeth move into position when the front teeth are damaged or fall out.

DOLPHIN

A playful, intelligent animal, the dolphin has a bottle-shaped beak and a happy expression that shows its friendly nature.

1

2

3

OCEAN BASICS

As the world's second fastest growing plant, kelp (or seaweed) grows up to 2 feet (.6 m) per day. This super plant is used in a lot of everyday products, including lipstick, ketchup, and ice cream!

FUN FACT

If you ever see a dolphin with one eye closed underwater, chances are it's sleeping! Because a dolphin can stay underwater for only 10 minutes before returning to the surface for air, it has to remain somewhat awake at all times. As a result, only one-half of the brain—and one eye—sleeps at one time!

EEL

With its single fin and slithery, snakelike shape, this creature is hard to mistake! Use long, S-shaped lines to draw the eel.

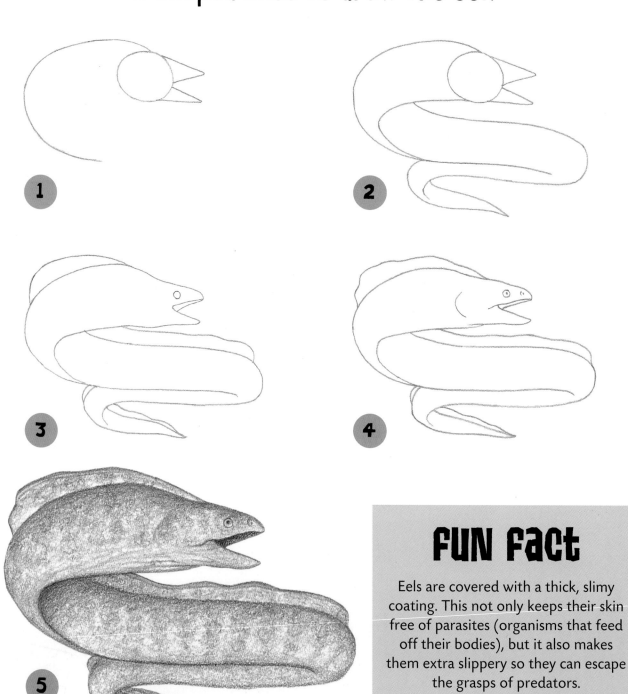

FUN FACT

Eels are covered with a thick, slimy coating. This not only keeps their skin free of parasites (organisms that feed off their bodies), but it also makes them extra slippery so they can escape the grasps of predators.

sea Turtle

Begin drawing this shelled sea creature using a small circle for the head and an egg shape for the body.

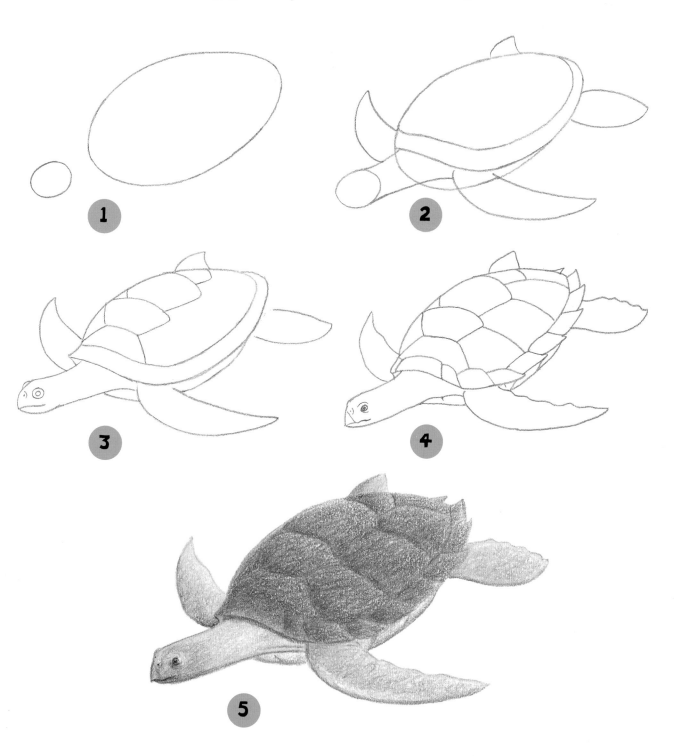

walrus

The walrus is known for its big, blubbery body and its huge tusks, which can be up to 3 feet (.9 m) long!

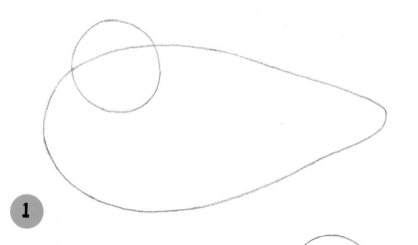

1

FUN FACT

Male walruses (also called "bulls") can weigh 3,700 pounds (1,700 kg)! As a result, they have to use their strong tusks to help pull themselves out of the water and onto the ice.

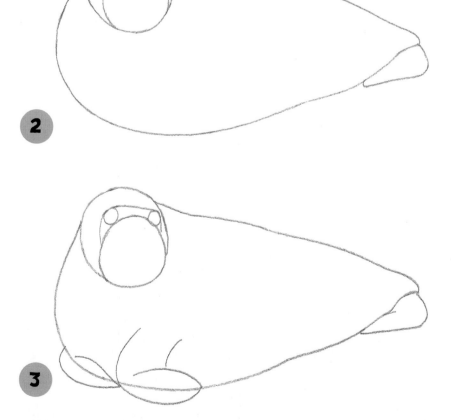

2

3

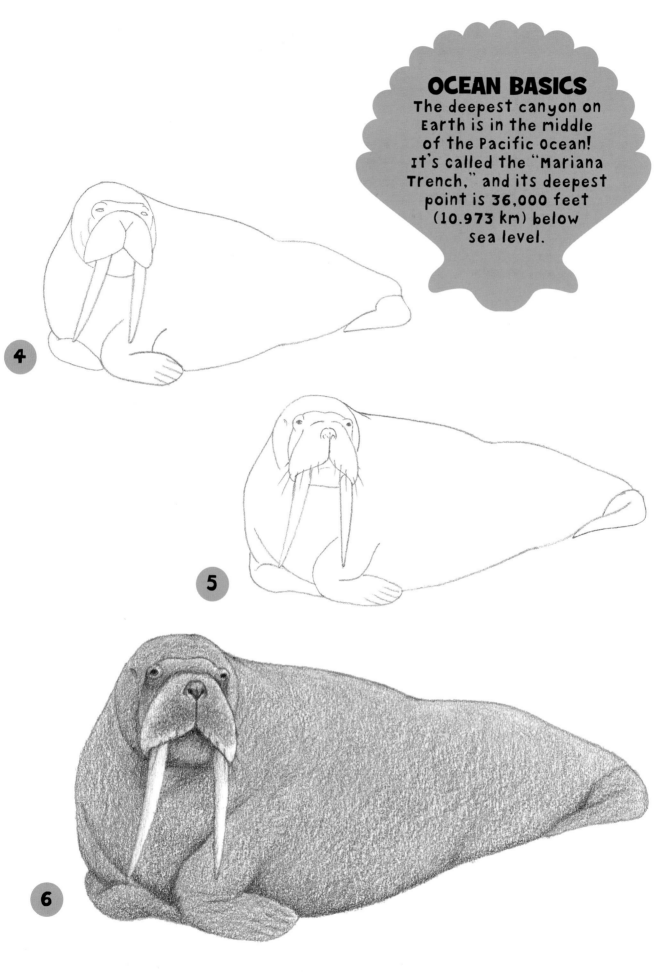

OCEAN BASICS
The deepest canyon on Earth is in the middle of the Pacific Ocean! It's called the "Mariana Trench," and its deepest point is 36,000 feet (10.973 km) below sea level.

4

5

6

JELLYFISH

A jellyfish looks like a bell with ribbons trailing behind it, but don't be fooled by its beauty. The "ribbons" are tentacles that sting!

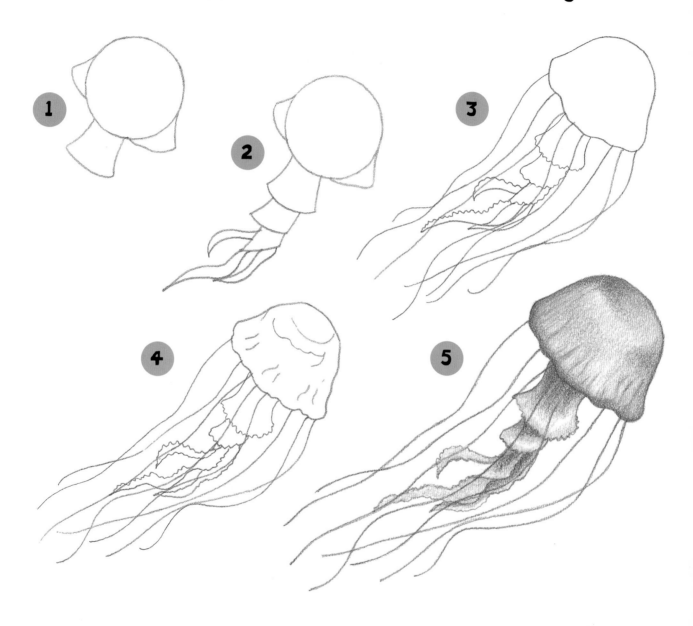

FUN Fact

The jellyfish has no lungs, gills, or internal organs for breathing. Instead it "breathes" through the thin walls of its body and long, stringy tentacles.

SWORDFISH

This fish's long, sharp bill resembles
a sword, creating a streamlined shape
that's perfect for speedy swimming!

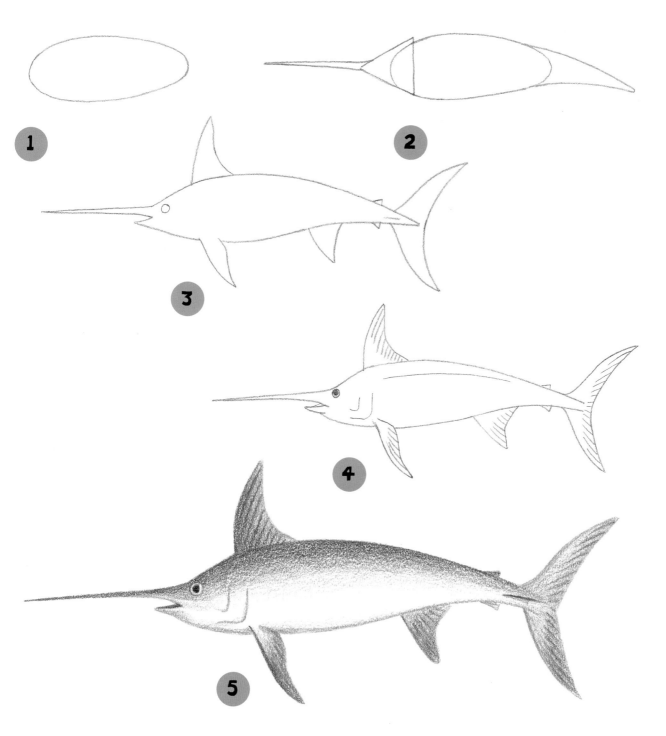

sea lion

start this sea lion with a circle for the head and an oval for the body. Then finish with a velvety brown coat!

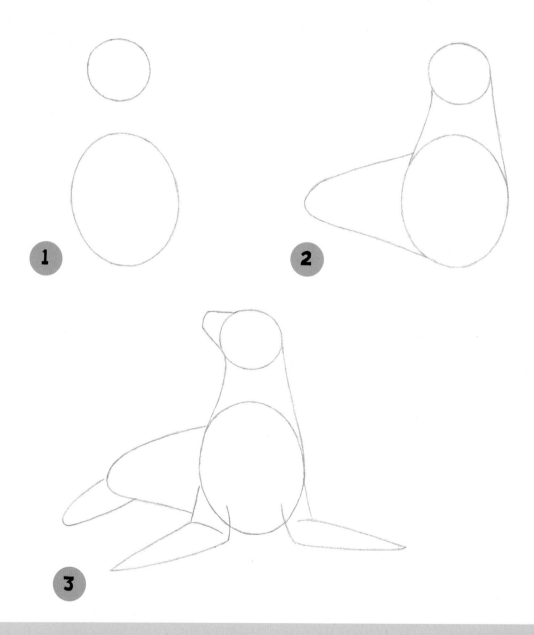

FUN Fact

When a sea lion swims, its front flippers push it forward while its back flippers steer. To help the sea lion move on land, the back flippers can also rotate forward under its body, acting as feet!

OCEAN BASICS

The average temperature of the oceans around the world is about 39°F (4°C)—only a few degrees above freezing! But water near thermal vents (openings that release heat from Earth's core) can be up to 400°F (200°C)!

4

5

6

Orca

The black and white markings on an orca— or "killer whale"—make this family-oriented animal easy to identify!

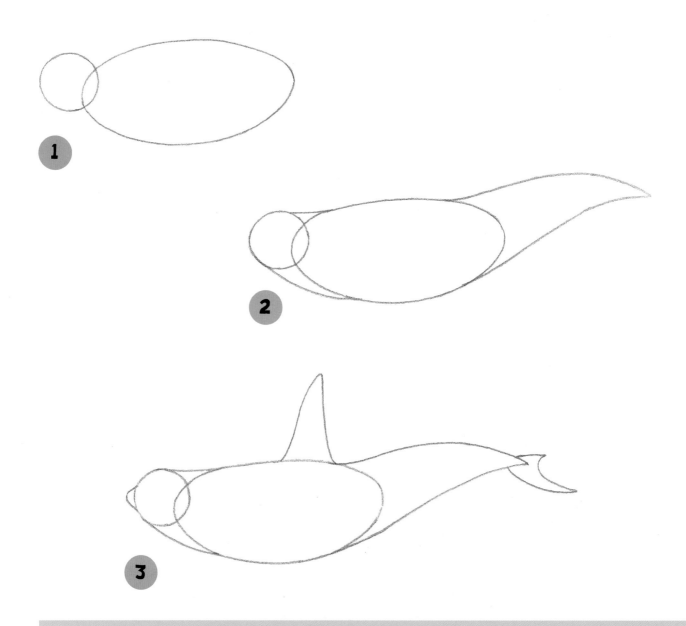

1

2

3

FUN Fact

The orca is an extremely skilled hunter, giving it the nickname "killer whale." It feeds on a wide range of prey— from small fish to blue whales—but a wild orca has never been known to kill a human being.

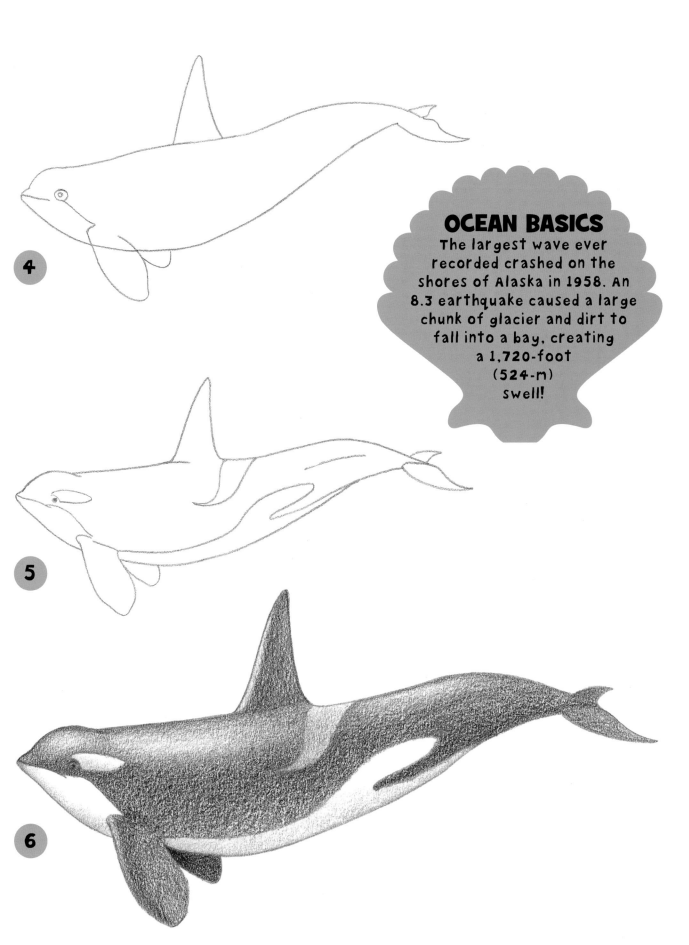

OCEAN BASICS
The largest wave ever recorded crashed on the shores of Alaska in 1958. An 8.3 earthquake caused a large chunk of glacier and dirt to fall into a bay, creating a 1,720-foot (524-m) swell!

HAMMERHEAD SHARK

This shark is named for its flat,
T-shaped head, and its eyes and nostrils
are located on opposite sides.

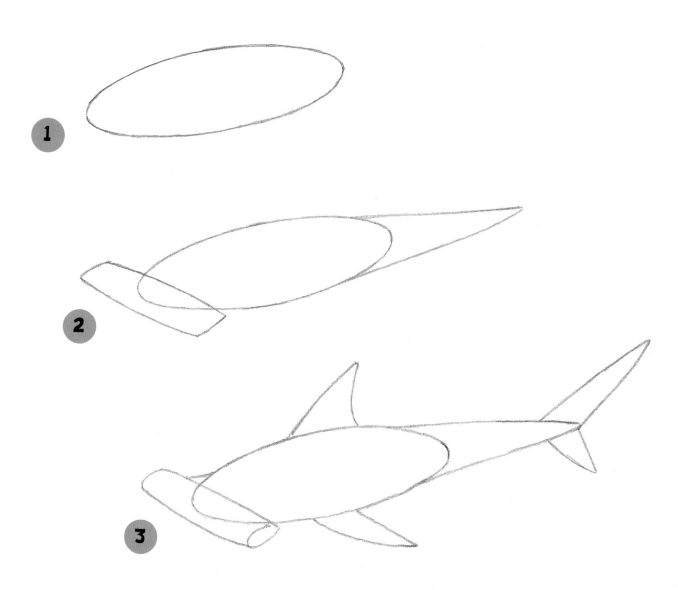

FUN FACT

Sharks have a sixth sense that humans do not. They can detect electrical fields around prey with organs called "ampullae," which help them find food in the dark ocean. Studies show that hammerheads have more ampullae than any other shark!

OCTOPUS

The octopus has a soft, oval body and eight arms covered with bubblelike suction cups.

FUN FACT

This animal doesn't just have multiple arms—it has multiple hearts, too! An octopus has three hearts: two for pumping blood through its gills to get oxygen, and one for pumping blood through its entire body.

seahorse

This unique fish has a horselike head; a spiky, S-shaped body; and a long, curled tail.

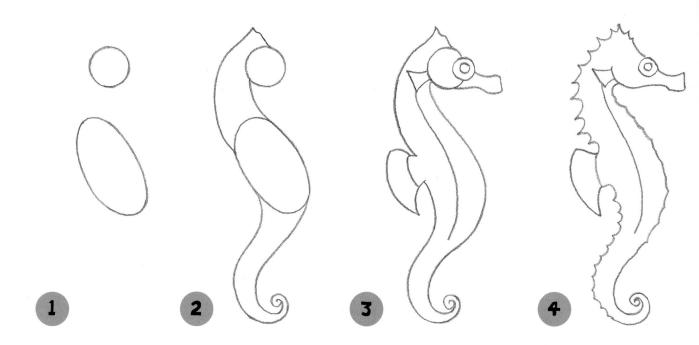

1   2   3   4

FUN FACT

Seahorses have a long, flexible tail that can curl around and grip nearby vegetation and coral. Because some seahorses are only 1-inch (2.5 cm) tall, they need their grasping tail to avoid getting swept away by the ocean current.

5   6